EASY PIANO

Arranged by DAN COATES

W9-BNZ-857

Product Line Manager: Carol Cuellar
Project Manager: Zobeida Pérez
Cover Design: Joe Klucar

Dan Coates® is a registered trademark of Warner Bros. Publications

© 2004 ALFRED PUBLISHING CO., INC.
All Rights Reserved   Printed in USA

CONTENTS

As Time Goes By 12

Back at One 8

Because You Loved Me 15

Foolish Games 20

God Bless the U.S.A. 24

The Greatest Love of All 44

I Could Not Ask for More 32

I Turn to You 3

I Will Always Love You 29

Lean on Me 36

My Way 40

Now and Forever 48

Over the Rainbow 51

The Prayer 54

The Rose 59

Somewhere Out There 62

Theme From New York, New York .65

There You'll Be 70

A Thousand Miles 80

Time to Say Goodbye (Con Te Partiró) 75

To Where You Are 86

Un-Break My Heart 91

The Wind Beneath My Wings 96

You Needed Me 101

Your Song 104

I TURN TO YOU

Words and Music by
DIANE WARREN
Arranged by DAN COATES

Slowly (♩ = 76)

I Turn to You - 5 - 1

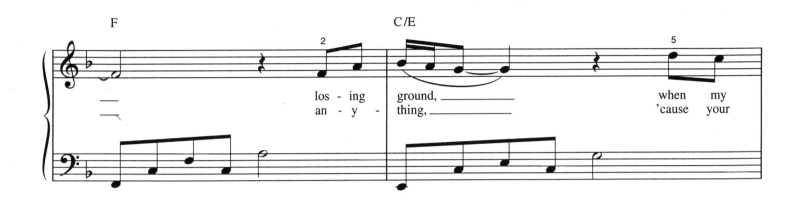

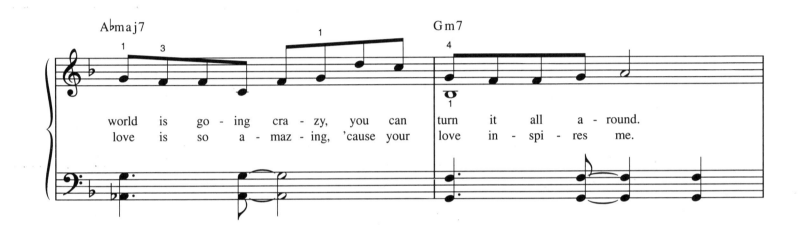

%. *Chorus:*

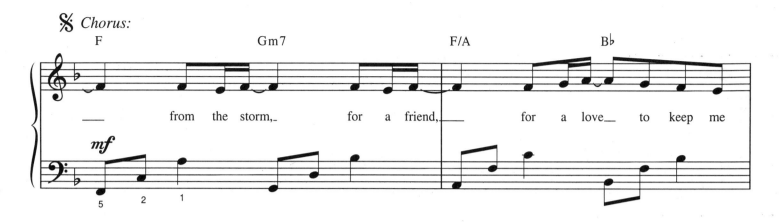

from the storm,_ for a friend,_ for a love_ to keep me

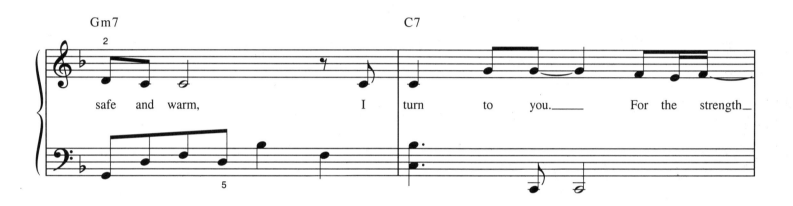

safe and warm, I turn to you._ For the strength_

To Coda ⊕

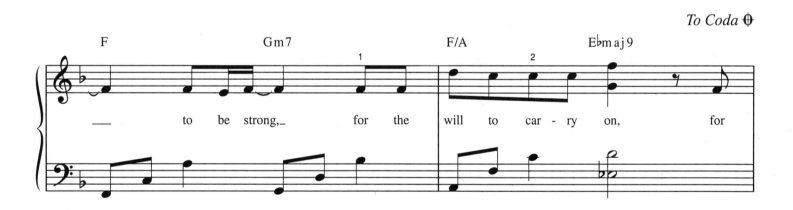

_ to be strong,_ for the will to car-ry on, for

1.

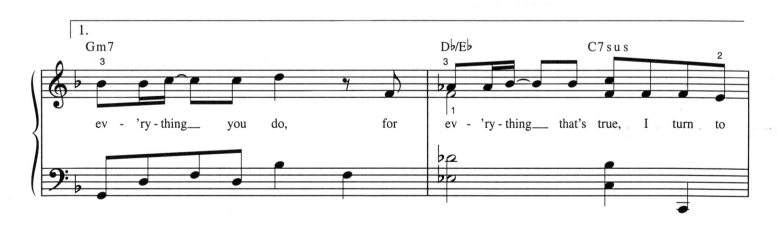

ev-'ry-thing_ you do, for ev-'ry-thing_ that's true, I turn to

Bridge:

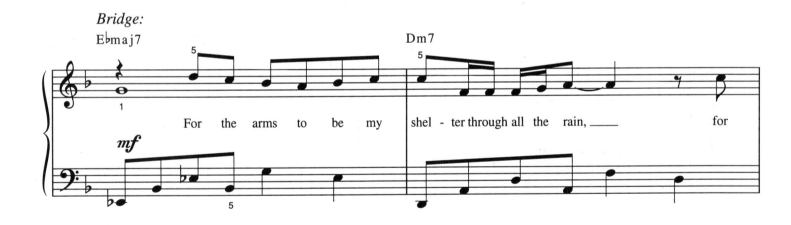

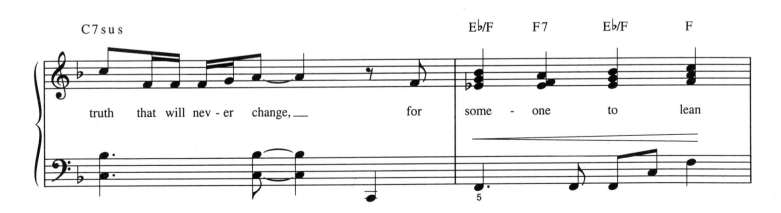

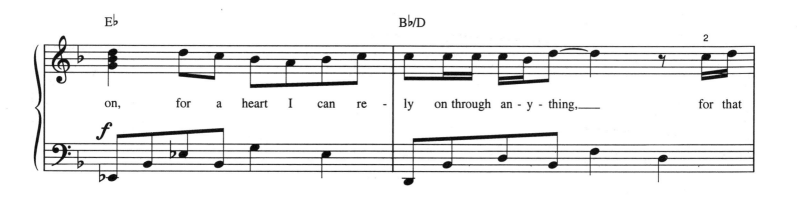

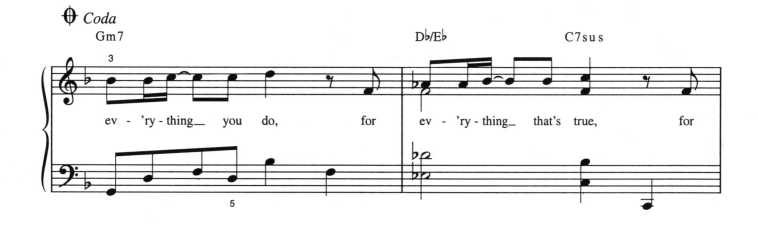

BACK AT ONE

Words and Music by
BRIAN McKNIGHT
Arranged by DAN COATES

Back at One - 4 - 1

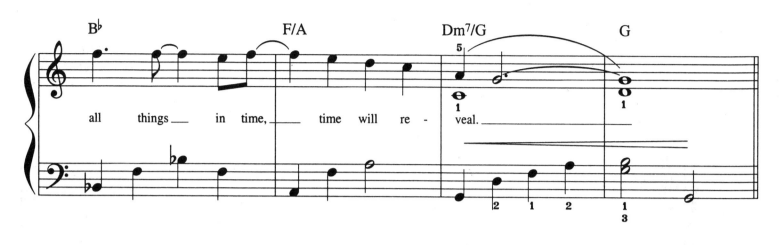

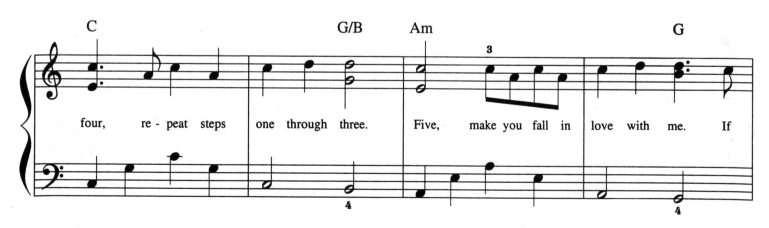

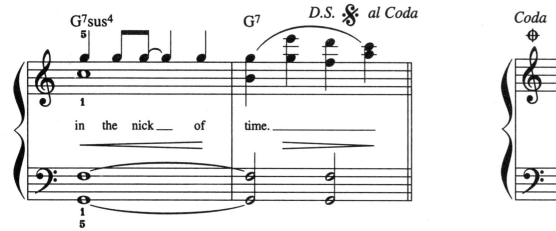

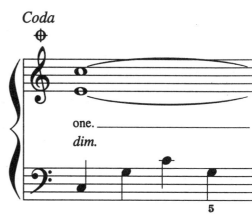

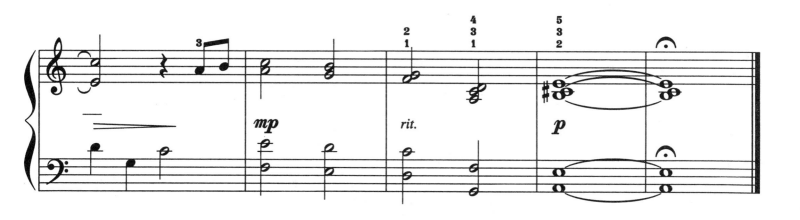

Verse 2:
It's so incredible,
The way things work themselves out.
And all emotional
Once you know what it's all about.
And undesirable
For us to be apart.
I never would have made it very far,
'Cause you know you've got the keys to my heart.
(To Chorus:)

AS TIME GOES BY

Words and Music by
HERMAN HUPFELD
Arranged by DAN COATES

As Time Goes By - 3 - 1

14

BECAUSE YOU LOVED ME
Theme from UP CLOSE & PERSONAL

Words and Music by
DIANE WARREN
Arranged by DAN COATES

Because You Loved Me - 5 - 1

FOOLISH GAMES

Words and Music by
JEWEL KILCHER
Arranged by DAN COATES

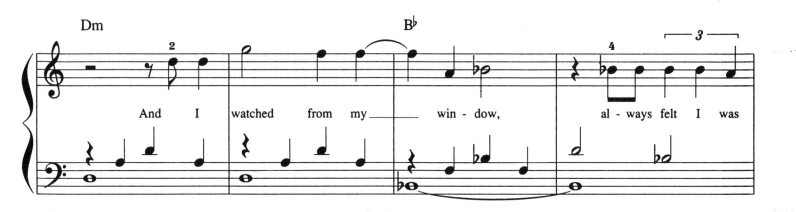

And I watched from my ____ win - dow, al - ways felt I was

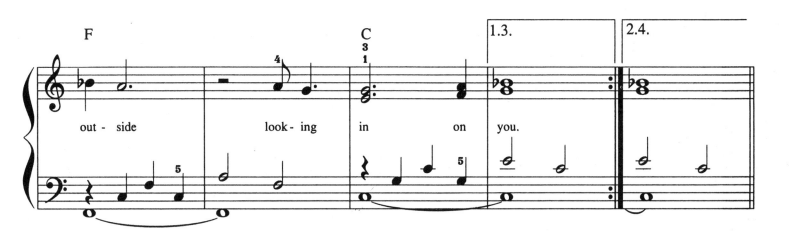

out - side look - ing in on you.

Bridge:

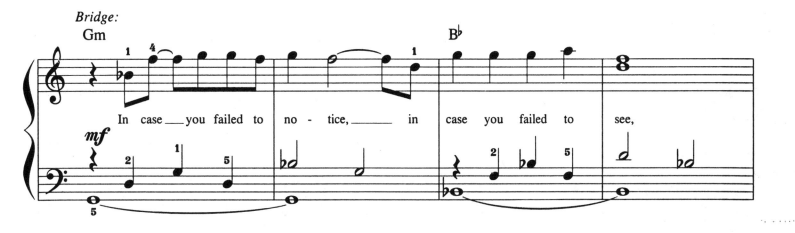

In case ____ you failed to no - tice, ____ in case you failed to see,

this is my heart bleed - ing be - fore you, this is me down on my knees.

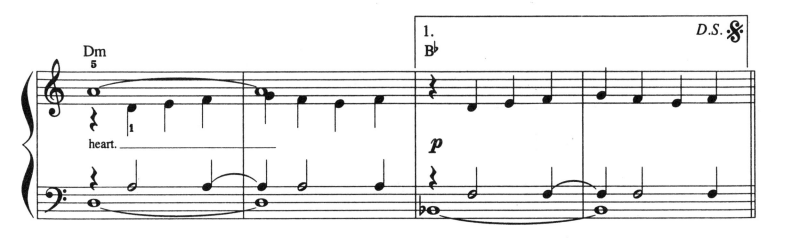

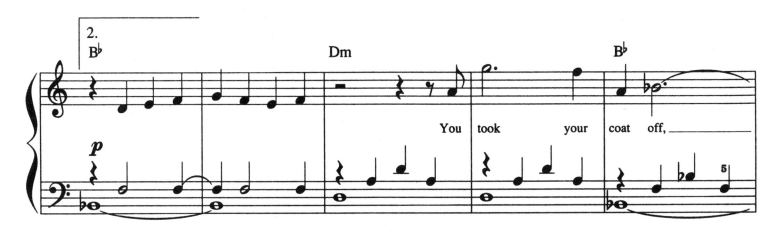

Verse 2:
You're always the mysterious one
With dark eyes and careless hair,
You were fashionably sensitive
But too cool to care.
You stood in my doorway with nothing to say
Besides some comment on the weather.
(To Bridge:)

Verse 3:
You're always brilliant in the morning,
Smoking your cigarettes and talking over coffee.
Your philosophies on art, Baroque moved you.
You loved Mozart and you'd speak of your loved ones
As I clumsily strummed my guitar.

Verse 4:
You'd teach me of honest things,
Things that were daring, things that were clean.
Things that knew what an honest dollar did mean.
I hid my soiled hands behind my back.
Somewhere along the line,
I must have gone off track with you.

Bridge 2:
Excuse me, I think I've mistaken you
For somebody else,
Somebody who gave a damn,
Somebody more like myself.
(To Chorus:)

GOD BLESS THE U.S.A.

Words and Music by
LEE GREENWOOD
Arranged by DAN COATES

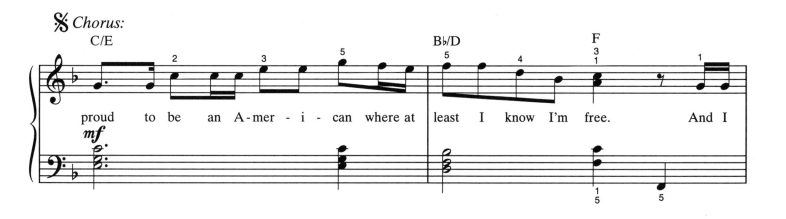

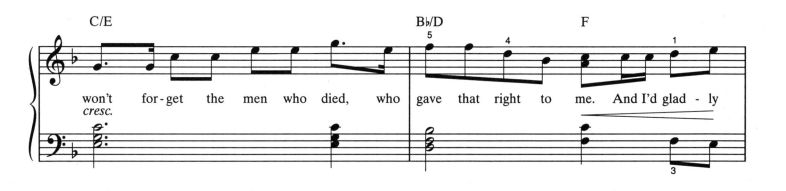

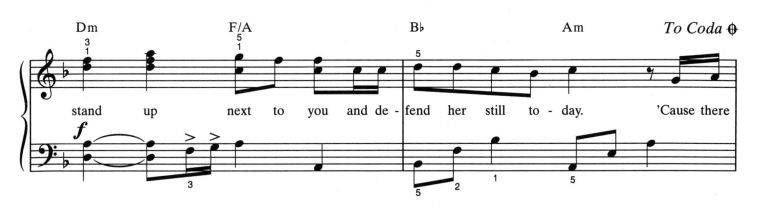

ain't no doubt I love this land._____ God bless the U. S.

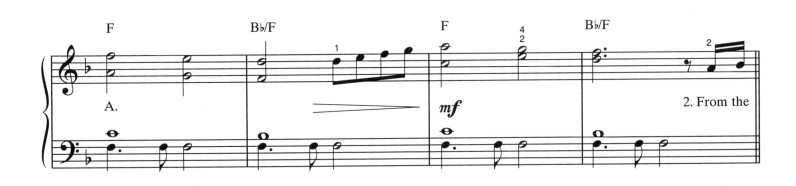

A. mf 2. From the

Verse 2:

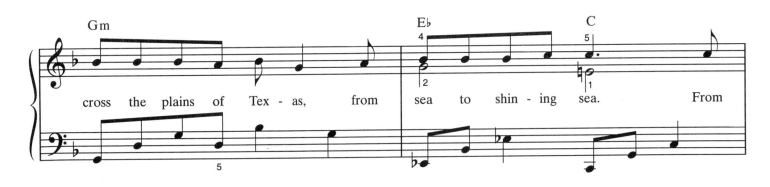

lakes of Min - ne - so - ta, to the hills of Ten - nes - see, a -

cross the plains of Tex - as, from sea to shin - ing sea. From

D.S. 𝄋 *al Coda*

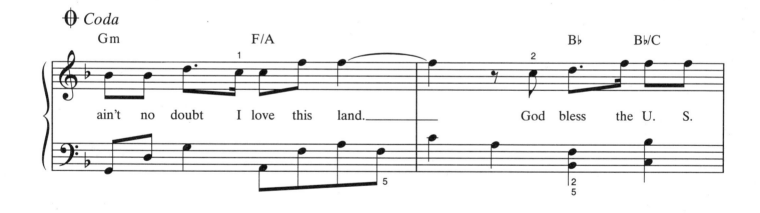

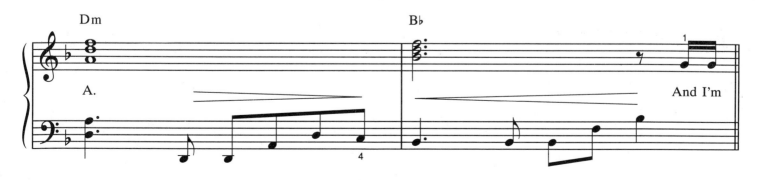

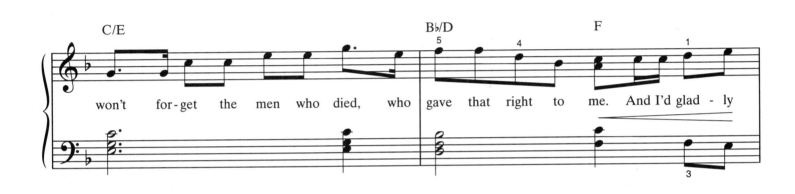

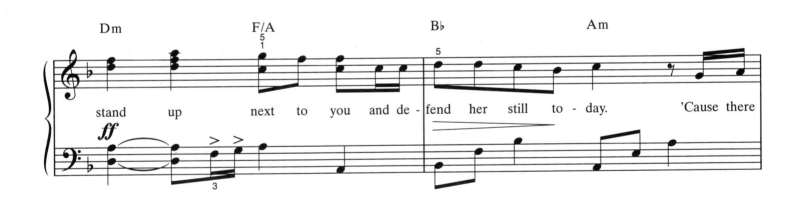

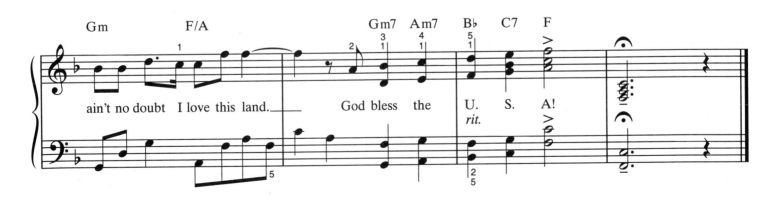

I WILL ALWAYS LOVE YOU

Words and Music by
DOLLY PARTON
Arranged by DAN COATES

30

I Will Always Love You - 3 - 2

Extra Lyrics:

3. I hope life treats you kind
   And I hope you have all you've dreamed of.
   I wish you joy and happiness.
   But above all this,
   I wish you love.

I COULD NOT ASK FOR MORE

Words and Music by
DIANE WARREN
Arranged by DAN COATES

Moderately slow rock beat

Verse:

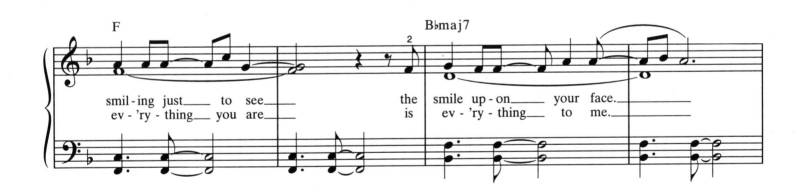

1. Lay - ing here with you, lis - t'ning to the rain,
2. Look - ing in your eyes, see - ing all I need,

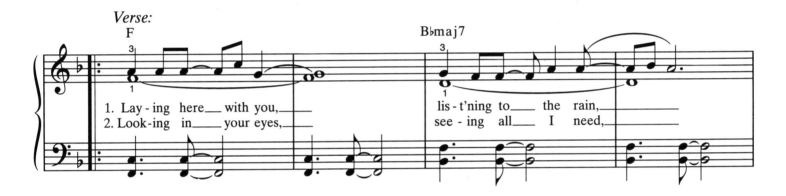

smil - ing just to see the smile up - on your face.
ev - 'ry - thing you are is ev - 'ry - thing to me.

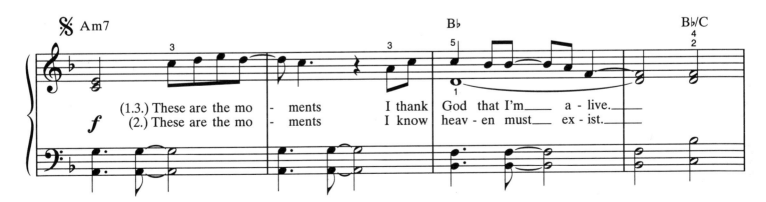

(1.3.) These are the mo - ments I thank God that I'm a - live.
(2.) These are the mo - ments I know heav - en must ex - ist.

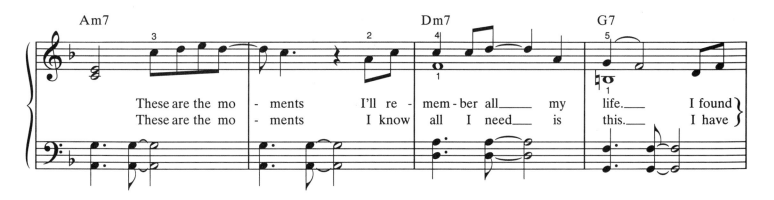

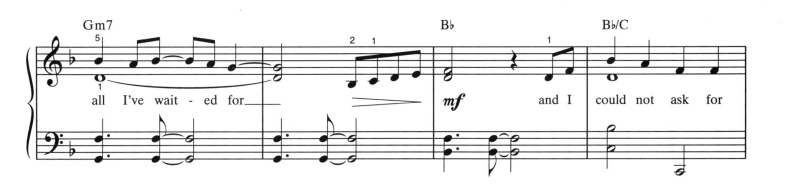

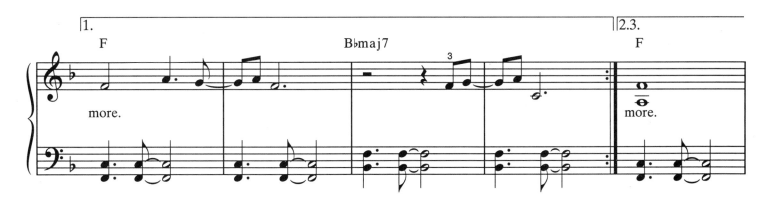

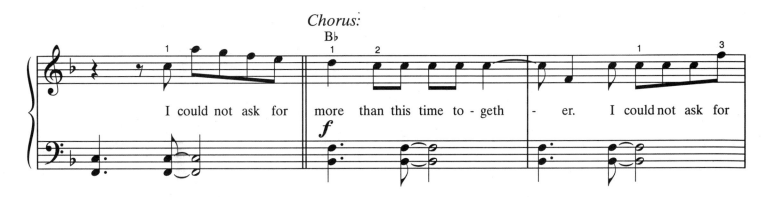

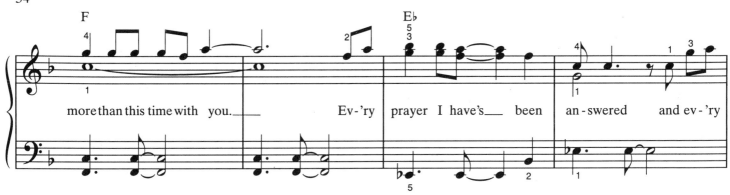

more than this time with you.___ Ev-'ry prayer I have's___ been an-swered and ev-'ry

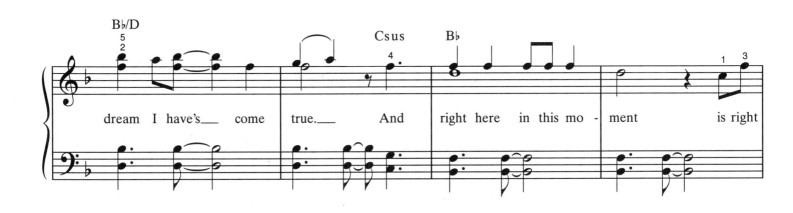

dream I have's___ come true.___ And right here in this mo - ment is right

To Coda ⊕

where I'm meant to be.___ Oh, here with___ you, here with___

D.S. 𝄋 al Coda

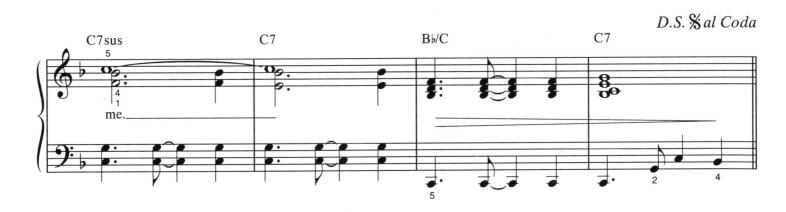

me.___

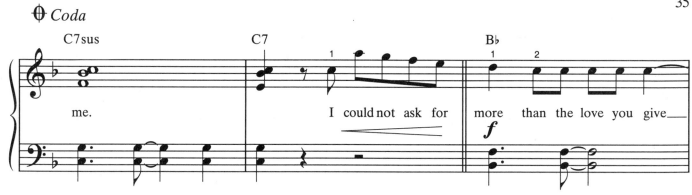

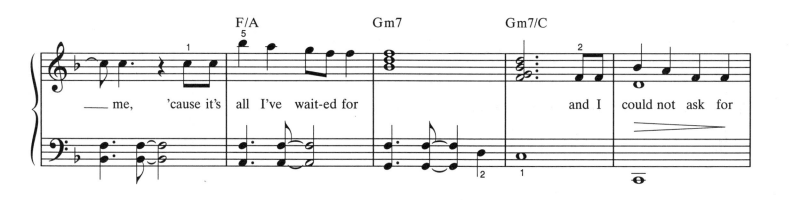

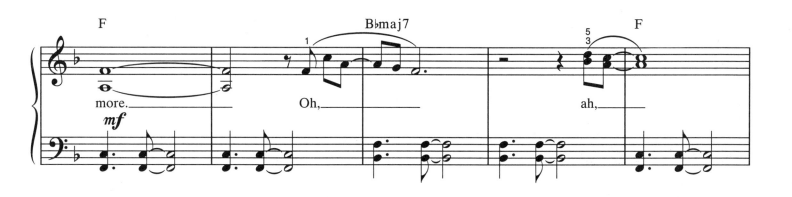

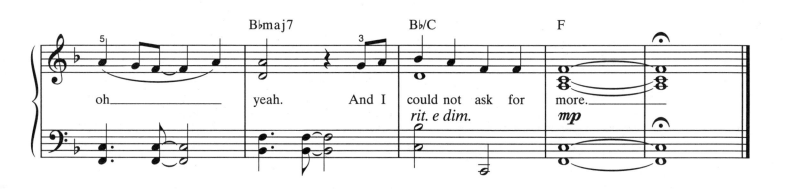

LEAN ON ME

Words and Music by
BILL WITHERS
Arranged by DAN COATES

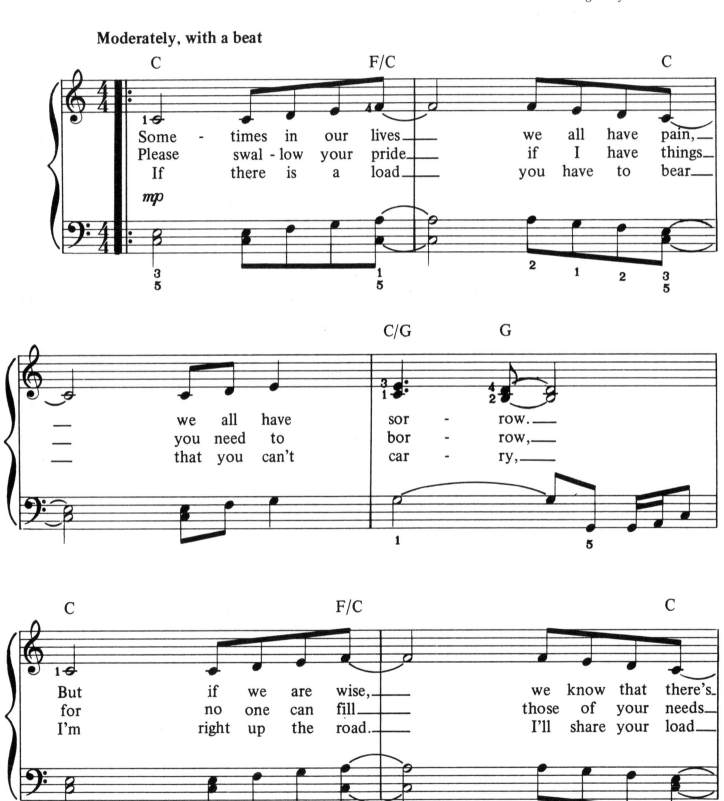

Lean on Me - 4 - 1

38

MY WAY

Words by
PAUL ANKA

Music by
JACQUES REVAUX
and CLAUDE FRANCOIS
Arranged by DAN COATES

42

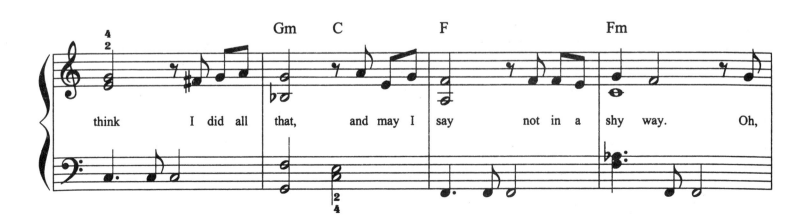

From the Columbia Picture "THE GREATEST"- A Columbia/EMI Presentation

THE GREATEST LOVE OF ALL

Words by
LINDA CREED

Music by
MICHAEL MASSER
Arranged by DAN COATES

46

NOW AND FOREVER

Words and Music by
RICHARD MARX
Arranged by DAN COATES

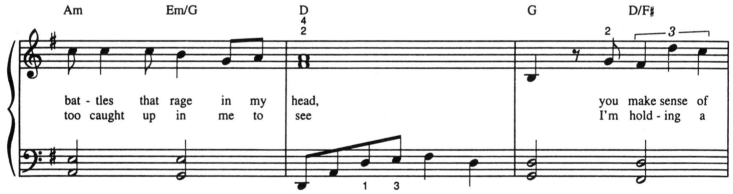

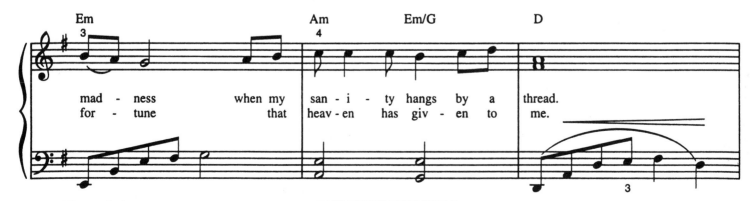

50

OVER THE RAINBOW

Lyric By
E.Y. HARBURG

Music by
HAROLD ARLEN
Arranged by DAN COATES

Over the Rainbow - 3 - 1

Over the Rainbow - 3 - 3

THE PRAYER

Italian Lyric by
ALBERTO TESTA and TONY RENIS

Words and Music by
CAROLE BAYER SAGER and DAVID FOSTER
Arranged by DAN COATES

The Prayer - 5 - 1

58

safe.
E la fe - de che hai a - cce - so in noi.

Sen - to che ci sal - ve - rá.
rit. e dim.

Verse 2 (English lyric):
I pray we'll find your light,
And hold it in our hearts
When stars go out each night.
Let this be our prayer,
When shadows fill our day.
Lead us to a place,
Guide us with your grace.
Give us faith so we'll be safe.

Verse 3 (Italian lyric):
La forza che ci dai
é il desiderio che.
Ognuno trovi amore
Intorno e dentro sé.
(Chorus:)

THE ROSE

Words and Music by
AMANDA McBROOM
Arranged by DAN COATES

The Rose - 3 - 1

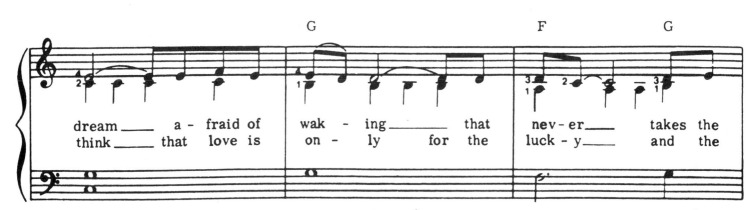

SOMEWHERE OUT THERE

Words and Music by
JAMES HORNER, BARRY MANN
and CYNTHIA WEIL
Arranged by DAN COATES

64

THEME FROM NEW YORK, NEW YORK

Words by
FRED EBB

Music by
JOHN KANDER
Arranged by DAN COATES

66

From Touchstone Pictures' "PEARL HARBOR"

THERE YOU'LL BE

Words and Music by
DIANE WARREN
Arranged by DAN COATES

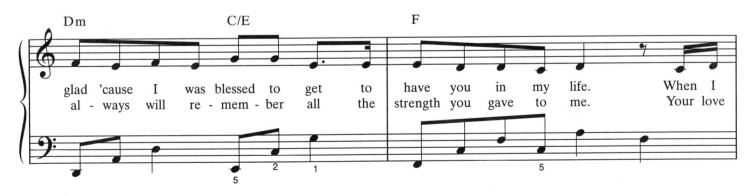

There You'll Be - 5 - 1

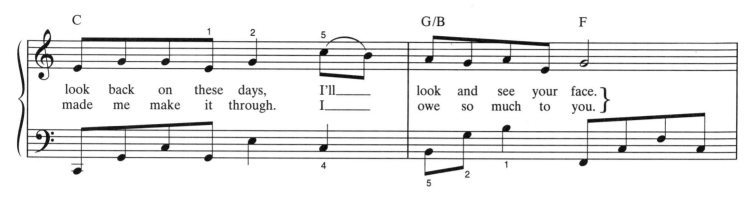

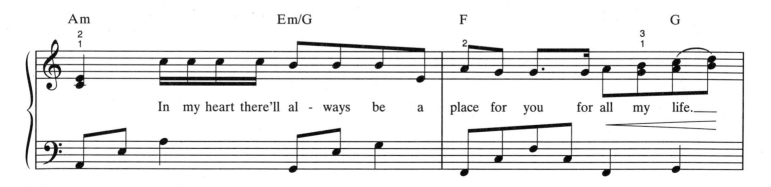

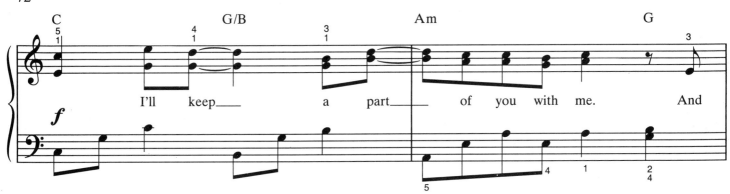

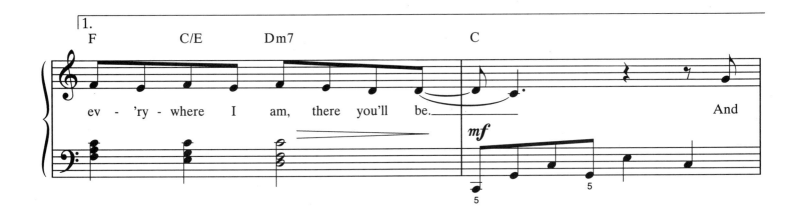

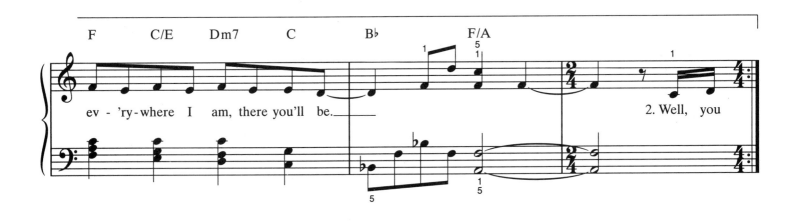

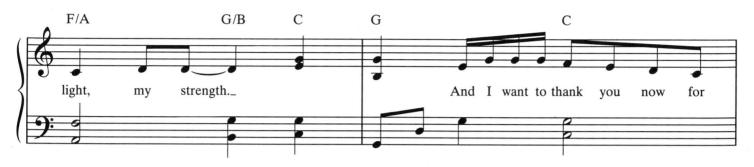

light, my strength._ And I want to thank you now for

all the ways you were right there for me._____

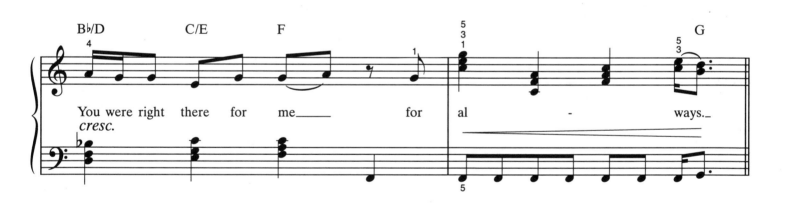

You were right there for me_____ for al - ways._
cresc.

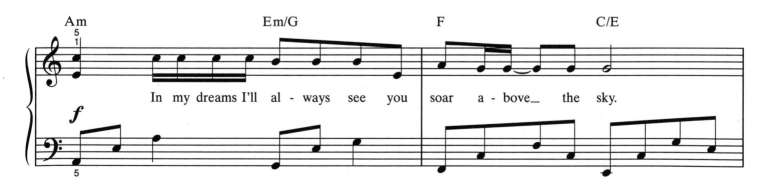

In my dreams I'll al - ways see you soar a - bove_ the sky.
f

There You'll Be - 5 - 4

74

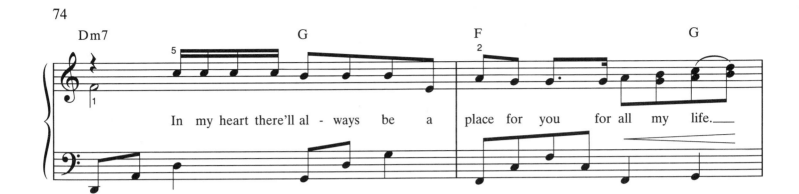

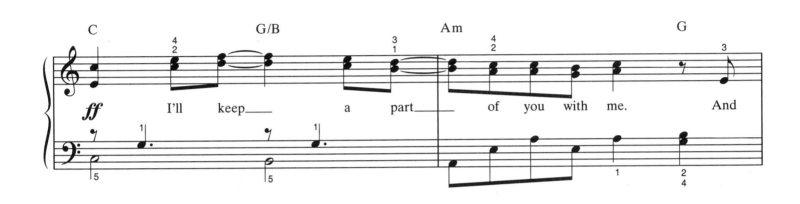

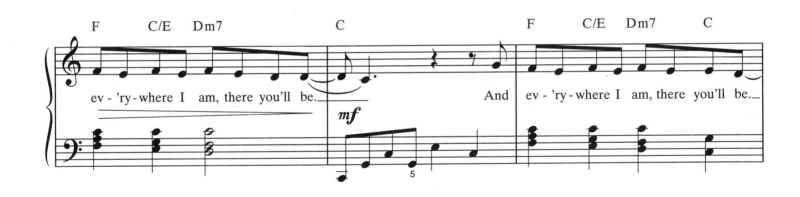

TIME TO SAY GOODBYE
(Con Te Partiró)

Lyrics by LUCIO QUARANTOTTO
English Lyrics by FRANK PETERSON

Music by
FRANCESCO SARTORI
Arranged by DAN COATES

Slowly

Verse 1:

Quan - do so - no so - lo so - gno_al - l'o - riz - zon - te_e man - can le pa -

ro - le, sì lo so che non c'é lu - ce_in u - na stan - za quan - do man - ca_il

Time to Say Goodbye - 5 - 1

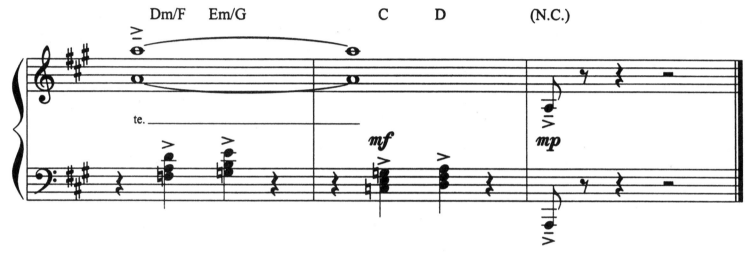

ENGLISH LYRICS

Verse 1:
When I'm alone,
I dream of the horizon
And words fail me.
There is no light
In a room where there is no sun.
And there is no sun if you're not here
With me, with me.
From every window,
Unfurl my heart,
The heart that you have won.
Into me you've poured the light,
The light that you've found
By the side of the road.

Chorus:
Time to say goodbye.
Places that I've never seen
Or experienced with you,
Now I shall.
I'll sail with you upon ships across the seas,
Seas that exist no more.
It's time to say goodbye.

Verse 2:
When you're far away,
I dream of the horizon
And words fail me.
And of course, I know that you're with me,
With me.
You, my moon, you are with me.
My sun, you're here with me,
With me, with me.

Chorus:
Time to say goodbye.
Places that I've never seen
Or experienced with you,
Now I shall.
I'll sail with you upon ships across the seas,
Seas that exist no more,
I'll revive them with you.

Tag:
I'll go with you upon ships across the seas,
Seas that exist no more,
I'll revive them with you.
I'll go with you,
I'll go with you.

A THOUSAND MILES

Words and Music by
VANESSA CARLTON
Arranged by DAN COATES

A Thousand Miles - 6 - 1

84

Verse 2:
It's always times like these when I think of you
And wonder if you ever think of me.
'Cause everything's so wrong and I don't belong
Livin' in your precious memory.
'Cause I need you,
And I miss you,
And I wonder...
(To Chorus:)

TO WHERE YOU ARE

Words and Music by
RICHARD MARX and
LINDA THOMPSON
Arranged by DAN COATES

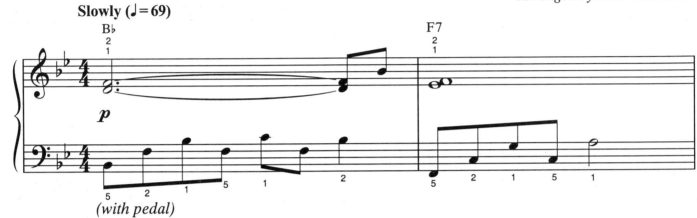

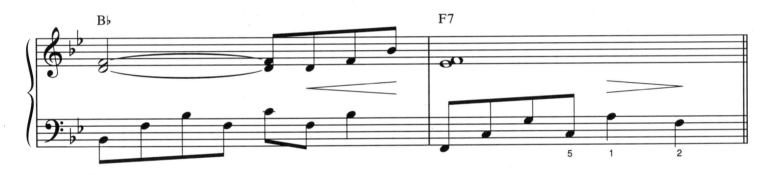

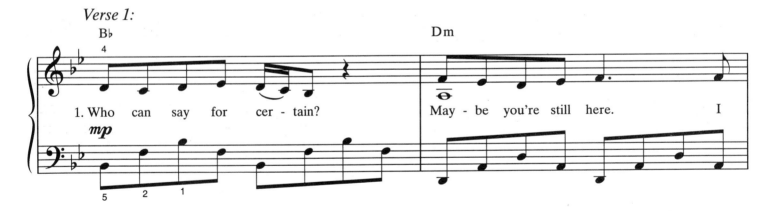

To Where You Are - 5 - 1

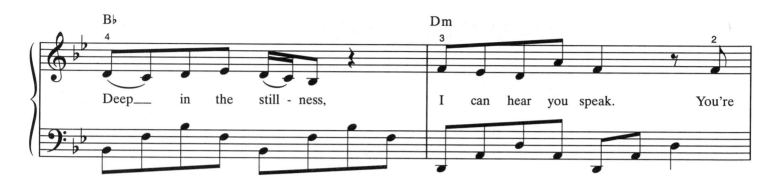

Deep___ in the still - ness, I can hear you speak. You're

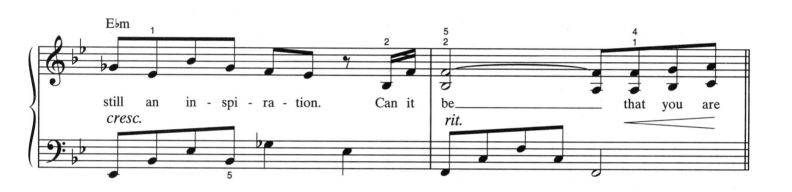

still an in - spi - ra - tion. Can it be_____ that you are

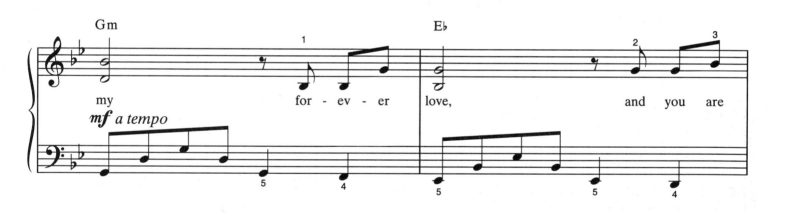

my for - ev - er love, and you are

watch - ing o - ver me from up a - bove?

UN-BREAK MY HEART

Words and Music by
DIANE WARREN
Arranged by DAN COATES

Un-break My Heart - 5 - 1

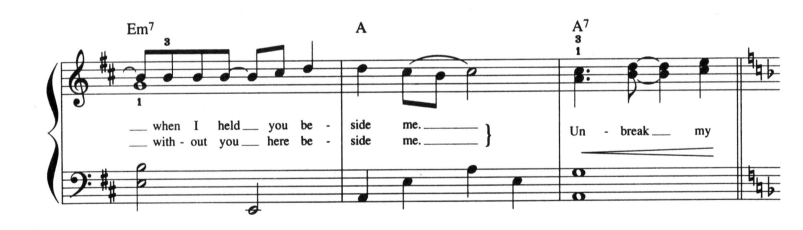

94

Un-break My Heart - 5 - 4

THE WIND BENEATH MY WINGS

Words and Music by
LARRY HENLEY and JEFF SILBAR
Arranged by DAN COATES

Slowly

1. It must have been cold there my
2. I was the one with all the

shad - ow,
glo - ry,

to nev - er have sun -
while you were the one

The Wind Beneath My Wings - 5 - 1

98

The Wind Beneath My Wings - 5 - 4

100

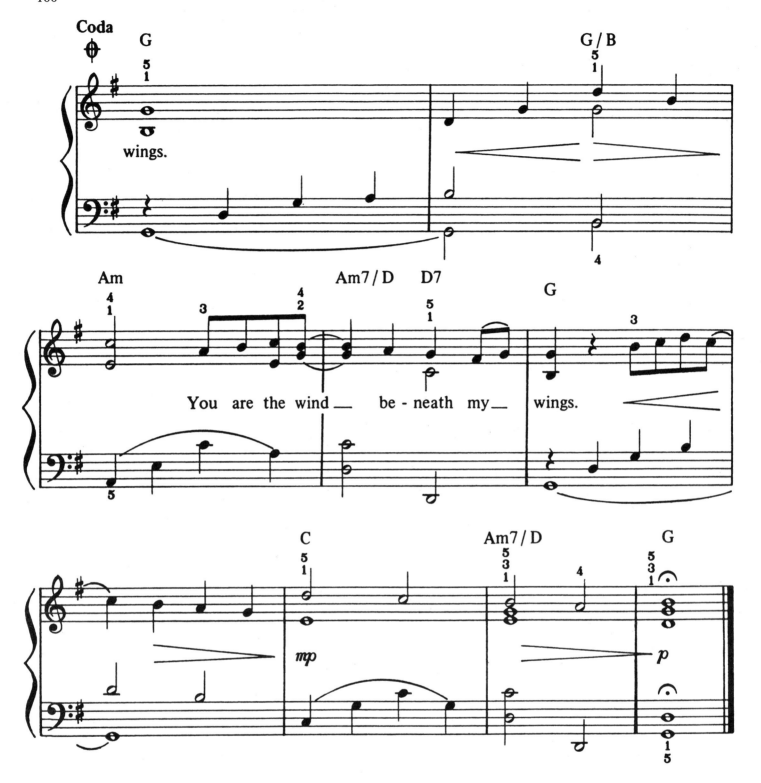

3. It might have appeared to go unnoticed
that I've got it all here in my heart.
I want you to know I know the truth:
I would be nothing without you.

The Wind Beneath My Wings - 5 - 5

YOU NEEDED ME

Words and Music by
RANDY GOODRUM
Arranged by DAN COATES

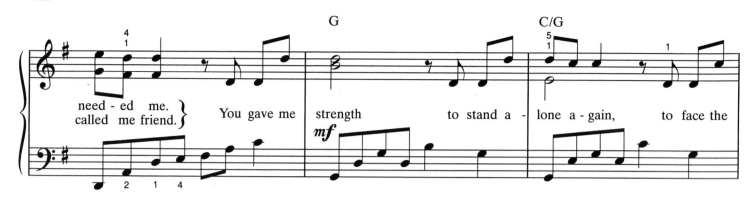

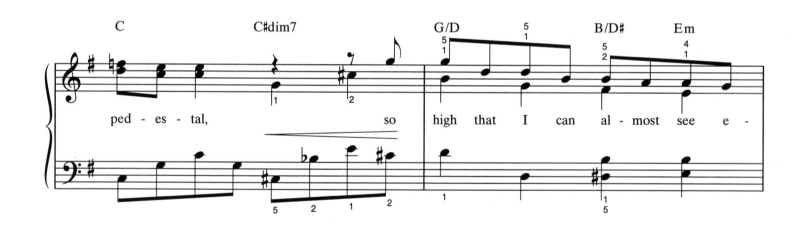

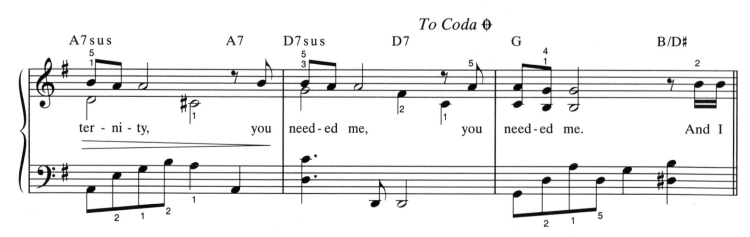

YOUR SONG

Words and Music by
ELTON JOHN and BERNIE TAUPIN
Arranged by DAN COATES

Slowly, with a steady beat (♩ = 64)

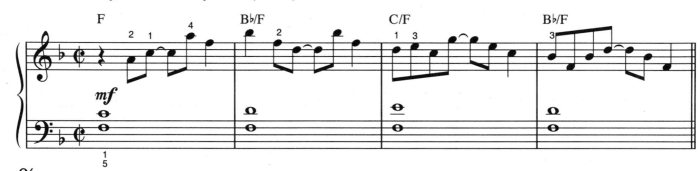

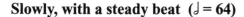

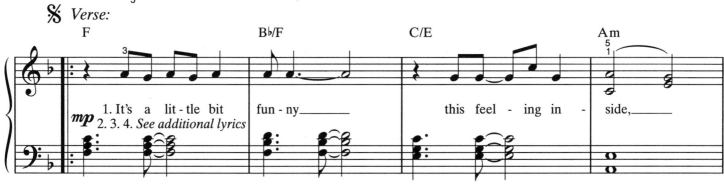

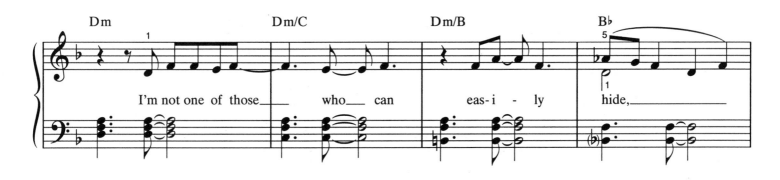

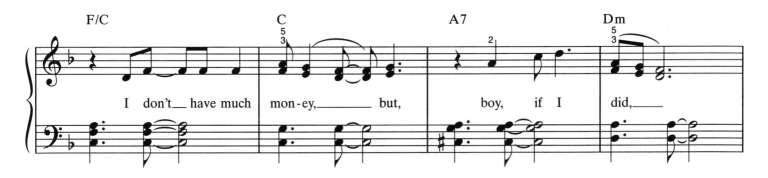

Your Song - 4 - 1

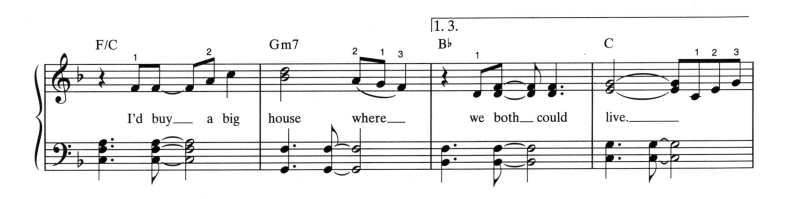

Chorus:

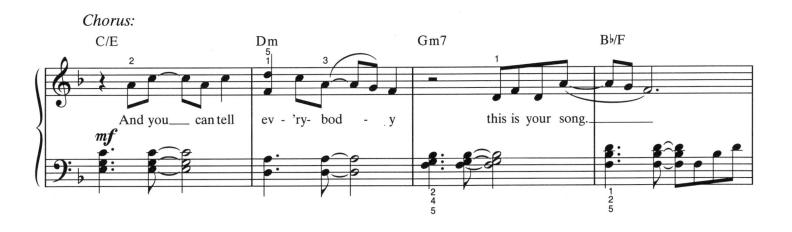

To Coda

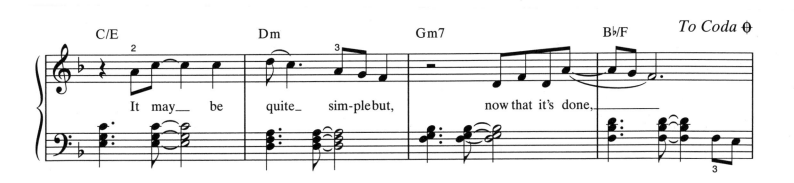

I hope you don't mind, I hope you don't mind that I put___ down in___ words how

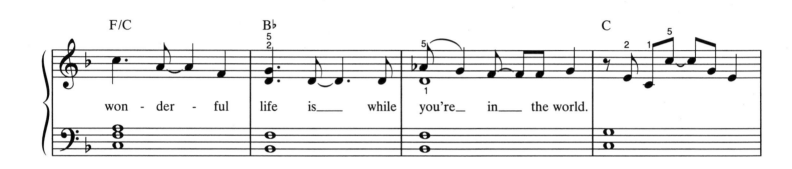

won - der - ful life is___ while you're___ in___ the world.

D.S. %̸ al Coda

Coda

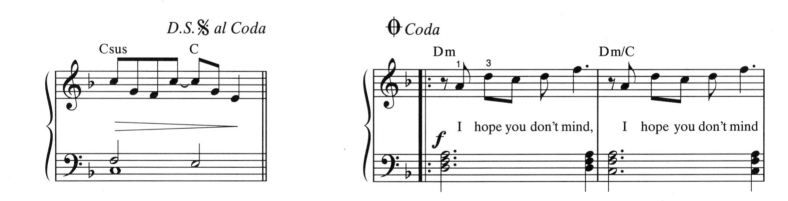

I hope you don't mind, I hope you don't mind

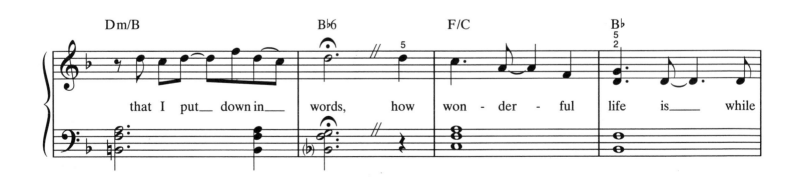

that I put___ down in___ words, how won - der - ful life is___ while

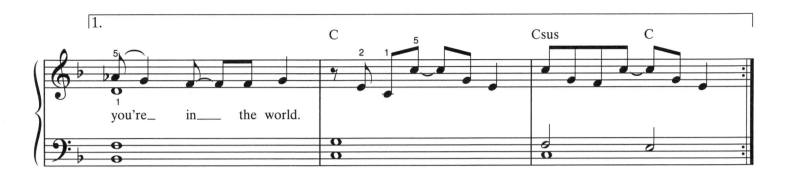

1.

you're_ in__ the world.

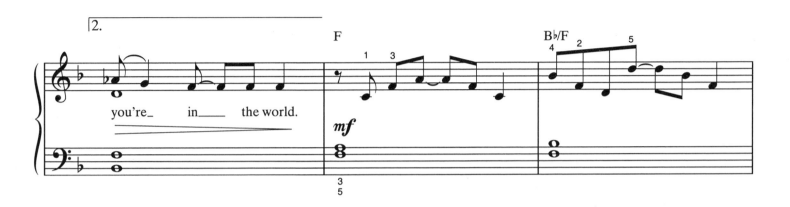

2.

you're_ in__ the world.

mf

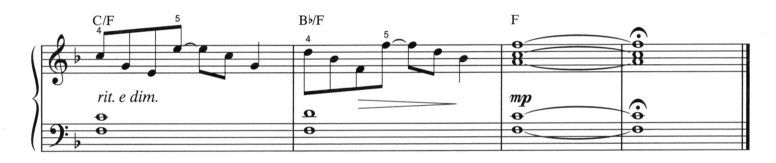

rit. e dim.

mp

Verse 2:
If I was a sculptor
But then again no,
Or a man who makes potions
In a travelin' show,
I know it's not much
But it's the best I can do.
My gift is my song
And this one's for you.
(To Chorus:)

Verse 3:
I sat on the roof
And kicked off the moss,
Well, a few of the verses,
Well, they've got me quite cross,
But the sun's been quite kind
While I wrote this song.
It's for people like you
That keep it turned on.

Verse 4:
So excuse me forgetting
But these things I do,
You see I've forgotten
If they're green or they're blue.
Anyway, the thing is
What I really mean,
Yours are the sweetest eyes
I've ever seen.
(To Chorus:)

Dan Coates

As a student at the University of Miami, Dan Coates paid his tuition by playing the piano at south Florida nightclubs and restaurants. One evening in 1975, after Dan had worked his unique brand of magic on the ivories, a stranger from the music field walked up and told him that he should put his inspired piano arrangements down on paper so they could be published.

Dan took the stranger's advice—and the world of music has become much richer as a result. Since that chance encounter long ago, Dan has gone on to achieve international acclaim for his brilliant piano arrangements. His Big Note, Easy Piano and Professional Touch arrangements have inspired countless piano students and established themselves as classics against which all other works must be measured.

Enjoying an exclusive association with Warner Bros. Publications since 1982, Dan has demonstrated a unique gift for writing arrangements intended for students of every level, from beginner to advanced. Dan never fails to bring a fresh and original approach to his work. Pushing his own creative boundaries with each new manuscript, he writes material that is musically exciting and educationally sound.

From the very beginning of his musical life, Dan has always been eager to seek new challenges. As a five-year-old in Syracuse, New York, he used to sneak into the home of his neighbors to play their piano. Blessed with an amazing ear for music, Dan was able to imitate the melodies of songs he had heard on the radio. Finally, his neighbors convinced his parents to buy Dan his own piano. At that point, there was no stopping his musical development. Dan won a prestigious New York State competition for music composers at the age of 15. Then, after graduating from high school, he toured the world as an arranger and pianist with the group Up With People.

Later, Dan studied piano at the University of Miami with the legendary Ivan Davis, developing his natural abilities to stylize music on the keyboard. Continuing to perform professionally during and after his college years, Dan has played the piano on national television and at the 1984 Summer Olympics in Los Angeles. He has also accompanied recording artists as diverse as Dusty Springfield and Charlotte Rae.

During his long and prolific association with Warner Bros. Publications, Dan has written many awardwinning books. He conducts piano workshops worldwide, demonstrating his famous arrangements with a special spark that never fails to inspire students and teachers alike.